Self-Defence for Non-Experts

a book for people who can't fight

Joe Bloke

ISBN-13: 978-1533113221 / ISBN-10: 153311322X

Contents

01. Does Anyone Need Another Book on Self-Defence?

02. Gauging the Danger.

03. Confrontations.

04. Pick Your Targets.

05. Men At Risk.

06. Women At Risk.

07. Domestic Violence.

08. Legal Implications.

The Inconspicuous Defensive Stance.

Eye Gouge.

Finger Break.

Front Kick.

Basic Punch.

Circular Elbow Strike.

Palm Heel Strike.

"The Old One-Two".

Sideways Elbow Strike.

Back Kick

Back Kick When Held.

Combining Simple Techniques.

Dedication

This book is dedicated to those who do not have anyone on their side.

"If you do not get it from yourself, where will you go for it?"

(Alan Watts)

Chapter 1

Does Anyone Need Another
Book On Self-Defence?

One evening two shodan (first degree) black belts in Shotokan karate were sitting in a bar having a drink after class. I was one of them. The topic of conversation was the fact that although we were "trained" karate men and would no doubt be called "experts" by people who knew nothing about the martial arts, we ourselves did not feel particularly safe in a dangerous world.

Oh sure, we were practicing self-defence techniques three or four days each week and as instructors we were teaching the art of karate to our students, who may well have seen us as skilled fighters. But that wasn't how we saw ourselves.

One of the first things you learn in any study of the martial arts is that it's really hard to actually land a blow on someone who doesn't want to be hit. Practicing with a willing partner who doesn't get out of the way might give you the false impression that you're getting pretty good at this fighting lark, but the two of us were not fooled. Actual combat, we realised only too well, was another matter.

We asked ourselves: which of the techniques that we practiced so diligently in our karate classes would we use if we were genuinely defending our lives in a real fight? In other words, which of our extensive catalogue of techniques would we be willing to gamble our lives on, and which would we discard as being unrealistic to attempt against an opponent who wanted to smash a glass bottle into our face or beat our heads in with a baseball bat?

We quickly concluded and agreed that we would never dream of using the flashy kicks and strikes that people usually associate with the oriental martial arts. In a *real* fight? We laughed out loud at the thought of trying to use the kind of showy techniques that are so beloved of martial arts movies. Head-high kicks? Ridiculous. Knife-hand finger strikes to the throat? Absurd. Are you kidding? It was obvious to us both that we would rely on the most simple and basic front kicks and straight punches. Forget about fighting like a so-called "expert" and focus on preserving your life and limb, that's what matters.

And so we happened upon the idea of writing this book. The purpose of what is written in these pages is to discard everything that a Hollywood superhero martial artist might do on the cinema screen and collect together some realistic advice with some realistic self-defence techniques for the *non-expert*. Who is the non-expert? Nearly everybody, we decided, including a couple of black belt karate men like ourselves.

When you think about it, this is the only reason why anyone might bother to write yet another book on self-defence. There are hundreds of books already available on the subject, all of which are much alike. In fact, they're largely interchangeable and they all seem to hold out the promise that you too can fight like the "experts".

This book is intended to be very different from all those self-defence books which have a picture on the cover of someone kicking someone else in the head. (Do you really think you can accurately kick a fast-moving target that high? In high-heels or after a heavy meal, not to mention after a few drinks?) Or the kind of books with a picture on the cover of a tiny woman physically dominating a huge man with some clever pressure point technique. (Have you ever tried finding a pressure point on an assailant who's wearing a bulky jacket? Or while his mate is attacking you from behind?) Or the type of book that advertises "secret" techniques and special "tricks" to keep you safe. The idea that there is a secret store of semi-mystical techniques from the Orient that provide you with almost magical abilities derived from the wisdom of the ancients has long been an appealing fantasy among westerners.

Self-defence manuals will often bombard the reader with a huge catalogue of set-piece techniques described in terms of "he does this / you do that". They provide an impressive directory of wrist-locks, blocking and trapping combinations, leg sweeps combined with restraining holds, and so on. They contain, let's be fair, a great treasury of combat knowledge. Complete with glossy photographs these elaborate manoeuvres can look exciting and inspiring to the uninitiated, and perhaps that is the point. They create the impression of considerable expertise on behalf of the authors, and of value for money on behalf of the readers.

But the problem with that approach is as simple as it is devastating. It can be expressed in two words: *reaction time*. Performing such techniques when you know what attack is about to be thrown at you is relatively easy. It is quite different when you have no idea what attack is going to be made against you. When the attack might come low or high, might be a fist or a foot, might come from the left or the right, might come singly or in combination, then the defender must take a moment to recognise the specific type of attack that is coming at them before they can attempt to apply their rehearsed defence against it. Unfortunately, that moment may be long enough to be fatal.

It takes years of practice to be able to perform the appropriate technique, especially if it's quite complicated, in a spontaneous manner. To react without thinking and yet still respond with the requisite technique, and to do so at high-speed (the only speed that matters in a real fight), isn't something that a reader can get from a book. Will the non-expert be able to remember the correct technique when they actually need it to preserve their life and limb?

In contrast, this book suggests only very simple single techniques described in terms of "drive your elbow into his face like this" and "twist his fingers like this". They are basic and uncomplicated actions which might therefore be applicable in a fight against someone who is trying their damnedest to do you harm. If in the chaotic muddle of two struggling bodies you find that you have hold of his wrist, then your can attack his fingers. If your opponent is suddenly no longer in front of you but coming at you from the side, then you can attack their face with your elbow. These single techniques minimize the reaction time.

Logically, a self-defence book is not intended for people who can fight, it is for people who can't fight. So what's the point of including lots of fancy manoeuvres that require considerable expertise to perform? If you could react fast enough to perform those techniques at real-fight-speed, then you wouldn't need a book. This book is intended for readers with limited training or no training at all.

Consequently, at various points in the text the reader may find themselves protesting "but that's just common sense". Yes, *exactly*. Common sense may keep you alive whereas attempting to apply secret pressure point techniques and fancy tricks to *turn a beginner into an expert by simply reading a book* (!) will get you killed. I do not pretend that this book will turn anybody into an expert at anything. It is a book for non-experts who want to avoid ending up in a situation where they get the shit kicked out of them.

This book is also a little different to those which do attempt to take a common sense approach to self-defence but which seem to think that sensible advice includes things like "dress in loose clothing that you can fight in". Of what use is that when you're going out for the evening dressed up to the nines? Or when you're on the train travelling home from work? Are you going to wear loose clothing every day for the rest of your life? The sensible approach isn't to advise people to wear loose clothes, it's to emphasize the self-defence techniques that might work in any kind of clothing. You don't know what you might be wearing when a situation of violence suddenly flares up on a bus or in a fast-food takeaway, so learning techniques that don't work in a tight skirt or fashionable shoes might not be so very sensible after all.

One reason why this book was worth writing is that a false sense of security can get you into trouble. Confidence is an asset, but over-confidence can fool you into thinking that you can handle a situation that, guess what, you can't handle. Nature gave you the capacity to feel fear for a reason. Fear is nature's alarm bell and it might be wise to listen to it, don't you think? But don't surrender to it.

For most of us, if a self-defence technique isn't simple then it won't work. More complicated manoeuvres may *look* as if they would work. They may seem to work in a self-defence class with an obliging partner and no sense of panic. But real fights are messy and confusing and full of fright. Your assailant is not helping you to perform your rehearsed technique, they're trying to pound your face with their fist. What matters in self-defence is *effectiveness*, nothing else. Therefore I shall put no strain on the reader's patience by using any foreign terminology (gyaku tsuki and mawashi geri, etc.) or by using any oriental imagery (we will not swoop like a crane or beat our wings like a dragon). I'll include only techniques that can be done in tight jeans or by people who are overweight; by the old as well as the young. My concern, like yours, is to avoid waking up in hospital breathing through a tube and wondering what's broken.

One other consideration needs to be mentioned before we proceed. This book is intended for ordinary people so it is about **unarmed** self-defence. A guy in a gym once asked me why I bothered to study karate when all an assailant had to do was to pull out a gun; how could karate protect me from a bullet? My answer was to ask him a question: how many people do you know who carry a gun? He didn't know anyone who carried a gun (this was in England in the 1980s) so his criticism of karate was largely irrelevant to the actual circumstances.

However, times change (England has changed out of all recognition since the eighties) and different countries have different laws about the right to own weapons so the question by the guy in the gym is relevant to the general issue of self-defence.

I shall not be considering the use of weaponry in self-defence because the basic premise of this book is that you, the defender, are an innocent person going about your lawful business when someone else forces a situation of violence upon you. Some self-defence manuals will recommend improvising a weapon from whatever comes to hand. For example, a key held in the fist so that it protrudes between your fingers, or a nail file used as a small knife, etc. These improvised weapons can be very damaging to an assailant and therefore effective as self-defence. But this kind of improvisation is a very different thing to carrying a concealed weapon or planning the use of weapons.

In most places the law does not recognise a citizen's right to carry a weapon like a knife for the purpose of self-defence. Perhaps you are less concerned about the law than you are about saving your life. (You might have a point there.) But the carrying of weapons *blurs the moral line* between the perpetrator and the victim. To carry a weapon might take you a significant step toward becoming one of the aggressors that society has to protect itself against. If, with premeditation, you carry a weapon then you may forfeit your right to claim the status of an innocent victim. I'm not saying that this *is* so, merely that it *may* be so in some circumstances.

Let's compare this to the example of the person who keeps a ferocious dog which they claim is "for self-protection". If that dog attacks someone (e.g. an innocent jogger) then the owner of the dog is to blame. They are not justified in saying that "the dog did it, I didn't". The owner is personally responsible for the dog and the dog's actions. Similarly, if someone tries to punch you and you stab them in the throat with a knife, then the fact that you're carrying the knife "for self-protection" may have turned a violent encounter into a deadly encounter. The moral line between who is the perpetrator of a crime and who is the victim of a crime has been blurred. Yes, they attacked you but were they trying to kill you? Yes, you were responding to a violent attack but you came prepared with the means to kill someone. Your status as an innocent victim is at least *questionable*, not only legally but also morally. For this reason I shall not address the use of weaponry for self-defence in this book.

Even unarmed self-defence entails fighting techniques that are potentially deadly. The consequences of any fight can be very serious indeed. **Be very sure that the situation really warrants the use of physical force before you use it.** The techniques in this book are intended for situations when you, the innocent victim of a violent assault, have no choice but to defend yourself; where there is no option except to fight.

Chapter 2

Gauging the Danger

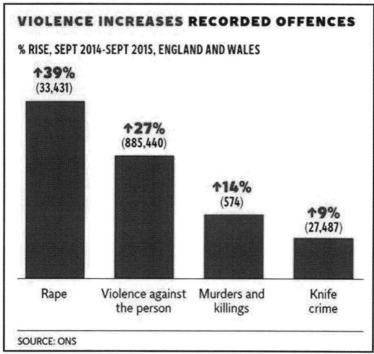

VIOLENCE INCREASES RECORDED OFFENCES

% RISE, SEPT 2014-SEPT 2015, ENGLAND AND WALES

↑**39%**
(33,431)

↑**27%**
(885,440)

↑**14%**
(574)

↑**9%**
(27,487)

Rape   Violence against the person   Murders and killings   Knife crime

SOURCE: ONS

Source: UK Office of National Statistics

I begin with this 2014/2015 graph of criminal violence in England and Wales not to scare you but as a reflection of what many people perceive to be the escalating level of the threat facing ordinary citizens in today's society. Here are government statistics on recorded offences of violent crime that appear to validate that perception. Everything is on the rise. Rape is *up* 39%, violence against the person is *up* 27%, murders and killings are *up* 14%, and knife crime is *up* 9%. England has come a long way since the genteel days of Agatha Christie novels about the body in the library.

You have just spent good money on a self-defence manual. Why? Because you are of the opinion that a time may come when you will have to defend yourself against a physical assault. You are right. Or maybe you've already suffered an assault and discovered that you couldn't handle it. So now you know that you need to be better prepared next time. But what is the actual level of the danger of physical assault?

If you're a drug-trafficking pimp for the Albanian mafia in London, you can probably expect frequent violence in your life, but what if you're a publican from Leeds? If you're a member of a gun-toting street gang in Detroit, then violence may be a daily reality, but what if you're a pharmacist from Wichita Kansas? If you're Jewish and you live near the Muslim banlieues of Paris, then your chances of meeting with violence will be extremely high, but what if you're a garage mechanic from Bordeaux? Regardless of whether the national statistics for violence are going up or down, it's difficult to judge accurately the threat of violence to ordinary peaceable people living their average lives.

The old cliché of violence is the gang of "youths" in the street assaulting passers-by. The new cliché of violence is the woman threatened by the man with whom she lives in her own home. We hear about bullying in the workplace and bullying in schools. We hear about cowardly students who insist upon "safe spaces" on their university campuses to which they can retreat when they are "triggered" by someone speaking words that make these weakling students feel "traumatized". Social media is full of unreliable messages about violence.

In today's society part of the problem is the discrepancy between perception and reality. This cuts both ways. Some people feel threatened when they're not, and some people don't feel as much under threat as they actually are.

Unfortunately, statistics don't tell the whole story. Governments like to downplay the level of the threat of violence by perpetrators who are strangers to the victim. After all, they don't want the electorate to think that the government is failing to protect its citizens. But at the same time the political class will exaggerate the prevalence of certain crimes where it serves their ideological interests. Women are not the main victims of violence in society but they are the main target of scary statistics about violence.

"Right now, nearly one in five women in America has been a victim of rape or attempted rape." [President Obama, February 8th 2015.]

In the present political climate there are innumerable research studies into rape but they produce widely varying results depending upon how the researchers choose to define the word 'rape'. Obama's statement was based on the 2011 National Intimate Partner and Sexual Violence Survey by the Centers for Disease Control and Prevention. It estimated that 1.9 million American women were raped in the preceding year. But another government research study in America, the National Crime Victimization Survey by the Bureau of Justice Statistics, estimated that there were about 350 thousand rapes in 2012. The figure of 1.9 million is more than *five times higher* than the figure of 350 thousand. These are both pieces of research funded by the American government but their findings are not even remotely similar.

President Obama chose to cite the research study that came up with statistics for rape and sexual assault that were five times higher. He could have chosen to cite the statistics that were five times lower. No doubt the scarier figure will help to prove the president's impeccable credentials as a feminist and "one in five" makes a good soundbite for the television news, but this kind of unreliable evidence doesn't help people to understand the real level of crime or the threat to themselves personally.

Feminist advocacy research seeks the highest and scariest figures it can get, and isn't above manufacturing statistics to suit its purposes. Feminist "research" may use self-selecting respondents (where women who haven't suffered rape are less motivated to participate in the survey), it will extrapolate national statistics from a small survey of local data, it will conflate rape with other forms of sexual assault, it will classify a woman who drank alcohol before having sex as being a victim of rape, and so on. (The Obama quote above was based on research whose definition of rape included "alcohol or drug-facilitated penetration" whatever that vague and ambiguous phrase is supposed to mean. Has any woman who had sex after smoking a joint experienced "drug-facilitated penetration"? Does that mean she was raped? If so, then male readers may want to remember never to share a joint, or a bottle of wine, with any woman they might want to have sex with later.)

I'm using feminist research as my example because it is such an egregious illustration of the unreliability of statistics. Feminist research will always treat what *women say* to the researcher as being the truth about *what actually happened*. If a woman ticks a box on a form to say that she has been assaulted, this by itself is taken as being proof that she was indeed assaulted. It is an iron rule of feminism that women who self-identify as victims must always be believed, so her unsubstantiated tick on a survey form is treated as *a fact* that a rape has occurred. There is no way to know whether the answers given to the research questions are true or not, but apparently this doesn't matter. The research findings will be quoted and re-quoted *as facts* by the mainstream media for years to come.

The same thing happens when feminist research asks women about whether they *feel threatened* in society. The research findings are often presented as evidence that women are actually under threat to the extent that they *feel* threatened, yet how threatened people *feel* may not reflect the truth of the true level of threat. As I said before, some people feel more threatened than they actually are, and some people feel less threatened than they actually are. Unfortunately, despite the lack of intellectual integrity in ideologically motivated research, it is always obediently believed by the mainstream media and publicised accordingly.

In stark contrast, male victimhood receives far less media attention. Societies, past and present, have always treated the protection of females as being of far greater importance than the protection of males. As the old phrase has it: "He's a man, he can take care of himself". Take Canada for example; nice, safe, well-behaved Canada. A country where, so the world likes to think, the men are all tall broad-shouldered lumberjack-types. Surely such manly fellows need have no worries about their ability to defend themselves from violent assault, if anyone were foolish enough to attempt it? Well, here is a picture of Canada that you might not recognise:

"In 2008 . . . men were more likely than women to be victims of the most serious forms of physical assault (levels 2 and 3) and have a weapon used against them. Men were almost twice as likely to be the victims of assault level 2 than women (215 versus 114 per 100,000) . . . . the rate of aggravated assault for men is over three times greater than that of women (18 versus 5 per 100,000). Young men under the age of 18 are 1.5 times more likely to be physically assaulted than young girls . . . In 2008, men were the victims of 80% of all reported attacks by strangers. Men were more likely to be robbed than women. They were victims in 65% of robberies in 2008 . . . Men were more likely than women to be a homicide victim, accounting for almost three quarters (74%) of homicide victims during a 5-year period between the years 2004 to 2008 . . . Men were 2.5 times more likely to be sexually assaulted in an institutional setting (school, non-commercial or non-corporate area) than women." [Government of Canada website, Victims and Survivors of Crime Week.]

I mention these extreme contrasts in the way that the media highlights female victims of violence and neglects male victims of violence because it graphically illustrates my point that the public perception of physical violence is very different from the reality of physical violence. This makes it more difficult for a person to gauge accurately the true level of danger that they face in society. The more statistics we seek out, the more confused and misled we may become. By way of another example, ask yourself which countries you would expect to have the highest number of criminal abductions (kidnappings). Columbia perhaps? Or Mexico or Haiti or Venezuela or India? Then consider the following:

"Which two countries are the kidnapping capitals of the world? Australia and Canada. Official figures from the United Nations show that there were 17 kidnaps per 100,000 people in Australia in 2010 and 12.7 in Canada . . . the high numbers of kidnapping cases in these two countries are explained by the fact that parental disputes over child custody are included in the figures. If one parent takes a child for the weekend, and the other parent objects and calls the police, the incident will be recorded as a kidnapping." [BBC News website, September 2012]

Are Australia and Canada *really* the "kidnapping capitals of the world" or are their statisticians defining "kidnapping" incorrectly? If you're a forty-three year old tourist visiting Australia, you probably don't have to worry much about being kidnapped, even if the country has very high figures for kidnapping. The official statistics may have nothing to do with whether *you* are in any particular danger or not. So whatever statistics you believe and whatever statistics you disbelieve, it's worth remembering that in the end your concern with self-defence relates to circumstances that *you* judge to be potentially dangerous for yourself or for those you wish to protect.

When looking at the graph at the beginning of this chapter (rape up 39%, violence against the person up 27%, etc.) one self-indulgence that you cannot afford is any reliance on the feminist rhetoric of "victim-blaming" which says "don't teach women how to protect themselves, teach men not to rape". Society has always had extremely harsh punishments for rape and expressed a massive social condemnation of sex crimes (even in prison sex offenders are targeted for punishment by other prisoners) so the message "don't rape" has always sounded loud and clear. The rhetoric about "victim-blaming" is naïve ideological idealism. Readers of this book will already understand this because to take an interest in self-defence is to acknowledge that you have some responsibility for your own security and you should take steps to protect yourself from becoming a victim.

Everyone, both women and men, are *accountable for their own actions* and that includes being accountable for taking reckless risks and behaving irresponsibly. From a self-defence point of view, there is no excuse for getting blind drunk in public and then claiming victimhood if something unpleasant happens to you. If you want to stay safe, don't get blind drunk in public. You are not a child, you are a responsible adult. It requires no great insight to realise that the most effective method of protecting yourself is to not get embroiled in a violent encounter in the first place. Hold yourself accountable for your own safety and behave with a mature sense of personal responsibility for yourself.

However, not even the most security-conscious person can ensure their own safety in all circumstances. Maybe you're the kind of person who stays on friendly terms with your next door neighbours, and always takes a taxi home at night in order to avoid walking home in the dark, and is careful not to drink too much when you're on a date, and yet trouble still manages to find you. You'll be in your car and you'll pull out into traffic and whoops! you've just cut in front of someone. The other driver screeches to a halt, leaps from their car, and starts berating you with a mouth full of road rage. Meanwhile you're thinking that if you lock your car doors they'll probably put a brick through your windscreen. The sad truth is that:

NO ONE IS SAFE

Sorry but there it is. It doesn't mean that the whole world is out to get you (even if it might sometimes feel that way), nor is it a defeatist policy advocating surrender. You don't need a self-defence manual to learn how to surrender. To recognise that *no one is safe* is simply an admission of what ought to be obvious, that any one of us might find ourselves on the

14

receiving end of a violent confrontation at one time or another regardless of who we are. So if you find yourself in a situation that you believe may turn violent:

THINK FIRST

Understand and clarify the potential danger. Are you genuinely at risk in this situation? Your antagonist may just be indulging in a lot of macho posturing. Don't see peril where there is none, for by over-reacting you may provoke it. A "siege mentality" may in some circumstances be justified, but paranoia isn't. You don't want to precipitate the very violence that you're trying to avoid.

ANTICIPATION IS GOOD, PRECIPITATION IS BAD

The three young guys standing in the street that you're walking down at night aren't necessarily going to start something. Or maybe they will. Be aware of the possible danger but do not prejudge. If you're a woman, do not assume that any man who stares at you is a rapist, even if feminism is constantly telling you that sexually predatory males are hiding behind every door. If you are a man don't assume that it's women who are the primary victims of violence and that you can deal with trouble if it starts. Don't allow false vanity to get you killed. Each set of circumstances is different. Each must be evaluated on its own distinctive features. How best the danger can be minimized or avoided may vary. There aren't really any definitive guidelines to follow that would apply universally. You need to exercise your own mature judgement.

Chapter 3

Confrontations

In a potentially violent confrontation you're not only confronting an opponent, you're also confronting your own fear. What you're feeling may well be written on your face for all the world to see. The importance of *mental attitude* both before and during an assault should not be underestimated. Aggressors are looking for victims. If your body language suggests that you are intimidated, then this may encourage the aggressor. You will *look* like a victim.

In contrast, an air of confidence may have the opposite effect. (Confidence is like sincerity; you may not feel it but you might nonetheless be able to fake it.) Your self-assurance may discourage the aggressor. They may decide to look for an easier target. So do not avoid eye-contact, but don't stare either as this may be taken as a challenge. (You don't want to get into one of those "who's going to blink first" contests that boxers always have at the weigh-in for a fight, making themselves appear ridiculous.) Stand upright and, if possible, adopt an image of nonchalance. Your demeanour just might sink you or save you.

You don't want to be unnecessarily intimidated by someone's tough guy appearance and attitude (rap music has filled the world with a lot of fake tough guys pretending to be boys from the hood, even though they live in Swindon and work at the supermarket) because that might mean that you defeat yourself before a blow has been struck. But, equally, don't make the mistake of underestimating your antagonist because you may allow yourself to be drawn into violence that your might otherwise have avoided.

It is true that bullies are sometimes cowards but, unfortunately, this is not true of all bullies. Some are hard bastards who use fighting as a source of self-esteem. They may not have anything else in their lives to feel proud of, but they feel great about themselves when they physically dominate another human being by physical force. For them, it's definitive proof that they are superior to you. Your pain and humiliation provides the bully with a fresh supply of self-respect. And, of course, his mates may be standing behind him, egging him on.

If and when a situation does escalate into violence, expect to be frightened. You almost certainly will be. Fear *isn't* the problem, *panic* is the problem. Fear may sharpen your senses and pump your adrenalin. But Panic will freeze your mind and make your physical responses slow and clumsy. At the very moment that you need to be acting decisively, you'll be bug-eyed and rooted to the spot, with your pounding heart trying to escape through your throat. You are a non-expert in a combat situation and you may be overwhelmed by the emotion of the moment. Panic makes you a sitting target. A dead duck.

Mental attitude makes a crucial difference because your mind may work *against* you. You're a peaceable person and you're not accustomed to violent confrontation. If you aren't used to it, violence is a shock. When it happens, it can happen astonishingly fast and leave you feeling unprepared. Which is why you are reading this book. You need to be prepared in advance. Once violence happens, there's no more time to think about how you got into this situation or why this antagonist is making trouble, and you can't afford the luxury of *distracting* yourself by worrying about it. There'll be plenty of time to ponder over the hows and whys of it when you're lying in your hospital bed. Instead of bewildering yourself with anxious questions about what caused this confrontation, you need to:

FOCUS ON THE PHYSICAL

Focusing on the physical begins with the positioning of your body so that you're ready to react physically should the antagonist attack you. But this doesn't mean raising your fists in a fighting stance because that is likely to provoke the

17

confrontation into violence. You're hoping that you might yet escape from this confrontation without having to fight. So what you need is to adopt an *inconspicuous* defensive posture. (Figures 1 to 3.)

The Inconspicuous Defensive Stance

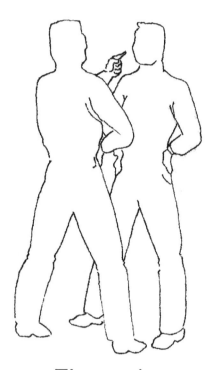

Aggressive and potentially violent confrontations are highly emotional and this can result in people adopting an "in your face" posture (Figure 1).

They puff themselves up to look big, pulling back their shoulders and sticking out their chest. This leaves them wide open if their antagonist were to make a sudden attack. In the worst cases, the "in your face" posture can include people thrusting their face forward and/or placing their hands on their hips.

This is a mistake.

Figure 1

Do NOT do this.

This posture makes no sense from a self-defence perspective. It's as if you wanted to provoke your antagonist into violence by offering them the first blow. It's an invitation to them to hit you while they have a wide open target in front of them.

Contrast it with the posture in Figure 2. This is not an overtly aggressive stance and although it looks relaxed it is far more defensible. Figure 2 is the *inconspicuous defensive stance*.

Your body is almost sideways toward your antagonist. One foot is drawn back so that you can put more of your weight on the rear foot to improve mobility. The rear arm offers cover to the abdomen and groin. The leading arm is casually placed across the lower torso ready to cover the upper body.

The intention behind this stance is to be ready to defend yourself whilst still being in a fairly ordinary posture which is not explicitly a fighting stance and therefore is not provocative.

Figure 2

Figure 3 compares the two stances. You can see that the angry "in your face" character is presenting a large target to his antagonist. His feet are not ready to move quickly and his groin is exposed to any sudden attack. The *inconspicuous defensive stance* offers a much narrower target and he has his hands at the ready, although it is still a posture that can pass for a "normal" way of standing.

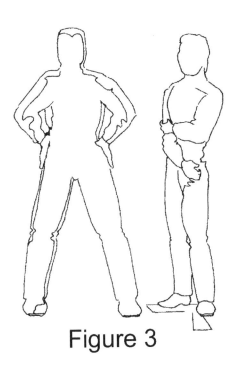

Figure 3

19

An inconspicuously defensive posture is clearly preferable in a confrontational situation.

Focusing on the physical also means making a rational self-assessment of the physical factors that may effect the outcome of this confrontation if it turns violent. Make a comparison between yourself and your potential opponent.

- What is your age compared to him?
- What is your height and arm-reach?
- How fit are you?
- How strong are you?
- How fast are you?

We will have to leave the question of how brave you are until such time as that characteristic has been tested. No one can know how brave they are without having found out the hard way.

If you are confronted by multiple opponents, then don't kid yourself. You're going to lose. You're not going to defeat three guys all by yourself. They're not going to take turns attacking you individually like they do in the movies. In real life they'll all rush you at once. (Why wouldn't they? It's their best chance of winning.) This is not a sporting contest, this is combat. You've got two fists, they've got six. If one of them jumps on your back while another one grabs your arm, how are you going to defend yourself against the third assailant? If they've got knives, your life is very seriously at risk.

This is where we have to forget all about those self-defence manuals which feature a lone defender dispatching one attacker with a kick to the head whilst simultaneously holding a second attacker at bay, who is subsequently dealt with by means of a series of moves which take two minutes to describe but which must be performed in less than two seconds. This super-heroic individual is not *you* and they're not *me*.

Rest assured, this superhero will not appear in a self-defence guide for non-experts. This book is a superhero-free zone. It cannot turn you into a lean-mean-killing-machine. Neither can those books which seem to suggest that they can.

A self-defence book cannot even promise to keep you safe, it can only offer advice. So here is a valuable piece of advice. Self-defence technique Number One is:

RUN AWAY

Self-defence is all about avoiding getting badly hurt. If running away achieves this, then running away is an important self-defence technique. It might not be what your favourite tough guy movie star would do, but you are not a tough guy and life is not a movie. Get real. We are less concerned with fighting than we are with surviving.

The trouble is, of course, that running away may not be an option. Your assailants may be able to *run faster than you*. If you're fifty years old and they're nineteen, how far are you going to get if you run? Or you may be confined in an enclosed space surrounded by furniture like the corner of a bar. Or standing in the checkout queue of a small grocery shop when some crazy guy who is between you and the shop doorway starts screaming at you for reasons you don't quite understand. Whatever the virtues of running away as a self-defence technique, it cannot be relied upon. So self-defence technique Number Two is:

TRY TO TALK YOUR WAY OUT OF IT

This is worth mentioning just in case it's still possible. Talking is safer than fighting. But if events have already reached the point where you're looking for a chance to escape by running away, then it's likely that they've already progressed too far for talking to do you any good. It's a solution that we should not discard while it's still an available option but, sadly, sometimes talking just isn't going to help. There are people who are fond of the idea that it is always possible to reason with an antagonist and talk your way out of any situation. This is not true. You know it isn't true. That's why you bought this book.

So we've now reached the point in our confrontation scenario where the only solutions are physical. These are the times when you can't run away and you can't talk your way out of it. Those times when you find yourself in a position where you have no choice but to defend yourself against a violent physical assault. Those times when it's a very good idea to have a few basic fighting tactics up your sleeve. So what do you do?

One thing you do *not* do is to put up your fists for a fair fight under Marquess of Queensberry rules. Your assailant(s) won't have read them, if they *can* read. No, what you need to do is to hit hard and then get out of there. The plan is simple: hurt them enough to disable them or otherwise dissuade them from continuing with the fight, and then remove yourself from the scene as soon as possible. The plan is to:

HIT AND RUN

This plan also applies to those scenarios where we are confronted by multiple opponents. If you are badly outnumbered, then the best you can hope for is to damage the first adversary sufficiently to intimidate the rest. If the first guy goes down hard, then the rest might have a change of heart. But failing that, you can only fight with a view to escape; to try to keep your assailants at bay long enough to make a run for it. But even against a single opponent, *hit and run* is a useful plan because it is a realistically practical goal. It has a fair chance of actually working.

It noticeably differs from what some people seem to think is the correct way to engage in combat. They are insistent that you must only make use of "reasonable force"; that you should only use the minimum amount of force required to keep you safe. But the problem with the concept of "reasonable force" is that it is *not reasonable*. Think about it. If you were greatly physically superior to your opponent, then you would be in a position to merely use the minimum amount of force required to constrain their attack. But if you were so superior to your assailant, then it's hardly likely that they would attack you in the first place.

We are concerned here with the ordinary person, the non-expert, the person who is not an effortlessly better fighter than their opponent. If you hold back from using your full force because you are concerned not to hurt your opponent too seriously, then you're foolishly increasing the likelihood that you will lose the fight. *You* are not skilled enough to have the luxury of taking it easy. You have to do whatever you can to survive.

This is why there will be no restraining techniques in this book. Restraining techniques are popular with the writers of self-defence manuals because "restraint" is favoured by the police who, from a purely legal perspective, endorse "controlling" moves and "holding" techniques. Such techniques inflict the minimum amount of damage to our assailant. (As if it were *their* safety we were worried about rather than our own!) But for the non-expert applying a choke-hold or a joint-lock on an opponent, should we be so remarkably lucky as to manage to apply one, does not achieve our objective. We have restrained our adversary and, for a few seconds at least, we have a secure hold on them. But do we actually want them?

Are we going to frog-march them seven miles to the nearest police station? Are we going to wait for the police to arrive, even assuming that there is someone else present who is willing to telephone them? (You can't phone because your hands are full.) How long can you control your struggling assailant before you get physically exhausted? As non-expert's we are not interested in restraining our opponent, we want to escape from the danger they represent to us. Restraining techniques are too ambitious for the non-expert. They are unrealistic. Remember to:

KEEP IT SIMPLE

As far as a policy of *hit and run* is concerned, "reasonable force" would merely mean that you stop fighting when your assailant is prepared to give up and let you leave. If you've done enough to protect yourself and leave, then you've done enough to have successfully defended yourself. In other words, it would not be reasonable to think "hey, I'm winning!" and proceed to beat your adversary half to death. You don't use so much force that *you* become the attacker, repeatedly kicking your helpless opponent in the head as they lay on the ground unable to defend themselves. It would be unreasonable to describe *that* as self-defence because you've already achieved your own safety.

But the fact remains that for as long as your own life and health are at risk from an assailant's attack, then as a non-expert you have to use your full force to defend yourself in whatever way is necessary. You cannot expect help. Don't suppose that strangers will miraculously rush to your rescue. You have to assume that you're on your own. Hit as hard as you can. Nobody wins on points. This is not a game. You'll have to be ruthless.

For the same reason, don't give your assailant any warning that you are prepared to respond to an attack. In a confrontational situation the advantage may go to the person who strikes first, so do not signal that you are ready to get physical. The inconspicuous defensive stance (illustrated above) will help with this. You want surprise to be on your side, not theirs.

If you are not ready on a hair-trigger to avoid an attack, then the assailant may connect with a surprise blow and while you're thinking "bloody hell, what just happened?" they are busy hitting you a second time. This is a serious consideration because when people who are not accustomed to getting hit are suddenly struck in violence, a common reaction is to freeze with shock. Another common reaction is to stumble away clutching at your face or whatever part of your body has just been hit. From a survival viewpoint, this is bad news. What's much worse is that if your assailant knows how to hit hard, then their first blow may be decisive. You fall down, and they start kicking you in the groin and stamping on your head. It may take quite a long time for the police and the ambulance to arrive.

Chapter 4

Pick Your Targets

Where you hit someone may be far more important than *how* you hit them. Think about it, what would hurt more and be more likely to dissuade an assailant from attacking you further: (1) a perfectly delivered punch to the stomach or (2) a clumsy but lucky elbow bashed into their eyeball? The sharp point of an elbow in the eye is probably going to do far more damage that a punch to the abdominal muscles.

Hitting a man in the chest may have little effect, especially if he is wearing a padded jacket that cushions the blow. But if you hit a female assailant in the breasts it could be a very effective deterrent that halts her attack upon you. When a person is struck on the shin it always hurts because the shin has very little muscle/flesh covering it, and shin-kicking doesn't require any skill. Any kind of kick will do.

Some people might think that kicking an assailant in the shin is not a "macho" or "heroic" way of fighting, but who cares? In a fight you're trying to hurt them to stop them from hurting you, so what does it matter if they suffer the pain in their shins rather than their stomachs? It only matters that *they* suffer the pain, *not you*. So hitting them wherever it hurts the most is a smart idea. If you can:

PICK YOUR TARGETS

For a male assailant the prime targets would include the eyes, the testicles, the shins, and the adam's apple (throat). These are all parts of the body that have no natural protection, i.e. they are not covered in muscle. For a female assailant the prime targets would include the eyes, the breasts, the shins, and the throat. The "balls and breasts" rule is worth remembering because these targets not only cause great pain, they also induce anxiety about permanent damage. Men really don't want to be hit hard in the testicles and women really don't want to be hit hard in the breasts.

Of course, by describing these vulnerable points as the prime targets I am *not* suggesting that you should aim for these targets *only*. When you're fighting for your life you should hit anything that you can make contact with because most of your attempts to hit your opponent will probably miss. It's frustratingly difficult to hit a fast-moving opponent and generally speaking you'll only be able to hit him when he's close enough to hit you. So you may have to settle for an exchange of blows; you'll have to take one to give one.

The thing to avoid is flailing your fists about wildly in the hope that if you just throw enough punches you will eventually hit something. This is a bad plan because you will get very tired very quickly. This wild fighting style is one of the reasons that most fights don't last long. To describe them in terms of athletics, fights are sprint events not long distance events. You will be burning nervous energy very rapidly. So having a few reasonably reliable techniques with which to strike your opponent and *aiming them at the targets which hurt the most* is a much better plan.

Just as hitting bony parts of the body can be usefully pain-inducing, hitting anything that bleeds can also be useful in dissuading an assailant from continuing. So the good old-fashioned punch on the nose should not be despised because it may cause a heavy nosebleed. If someone sees a lot of blood on their shirt and realises that it's their own blood, they may think that now would be an opportune moment to call the fight to a halt. If they do, then you've won. Remember, this is not sport, this is combat. You're not trying to win a prize, you're trying to win your safety. A fight is not about impressing an admiring crowd of spectators with your fighting prowess, it's about survival. It's about not waking up in the intensive care unit of your local hospital.

This is why we shouldn't be too pretentious about the methods we use to ensure our own survival. It doesn't have to be pretty and it doesn't have to be fair, it just has to work when we need it to work. Honourable combat may be appropriate for gladiators in the arena, but it's not so suitable for non-experts in the street.

Fighting for survival can be dirty and nasty. For example, it doesn't really require any training or skill to gouge someone's eyes, you just need to have the ruthlessness (or, frankly, the terrified desperation) to stick your thumbs into their eyes.

Eye Gouge

This is often taught as a double gouge (i.e. grabbing the sides of your assailant's head and pushing both your thumbs into their eyes) because it is employed as a way of breaking an opponent's hold on you. If they grab you from the front, gouging their eyes pushes them away from you. However, this technique may be even more damaging if you gouge only one eye and use your free hand to hold the assailant *behind* the head. This gives you more leverage to gouge and it is very nasty.

Another technique that doesn't require any training or skill is to grab one of your opponent's fingers (it doesn't matter which one) and jerk it straight back against the knuckle very hard. Your intention is to break the finger at the knuckle.

But when it cracks, *don't let go*. Hang on to that finger and wrench it about in all directions at once. This will cause excruciating agony. The pain may be sufficient to change your adversary's mind about the wisdom of continuing to attack you.

Finger Breaking

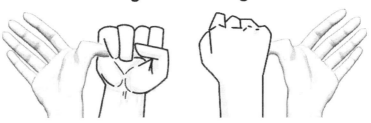

However, not all combat is so crude as gouging eyes and breaking fingers. Even simple self-defence needs practice. The techniques illustrated in this book will require practice to be performed effectively, but they are all simple enough for the non-expert to learn at home by themselves or with a partner. (Working with a partner is better if you happen to have a friend who is also interested in learning self-defence.) Learning anything of value takes time and effort, and the method to follow here can be summed up as:

REPETITION, REPETITION, REPETITION

When practicing these techniques remember that you're trying to embed these movements into your "muscle memory". You won't have much time for thinking in a real fight, so you need your body to react to an assault by producing these techniques spontaneously. The way to train this "muscle memory" is to perform very high numbers of repetitions. You have to repeat the movement over and over. Exhaust your muscles by repeating the movements until fatigue forces you to stop. Then try to keep on going with more repetitions of the same technique. The next time you practice, try to do more repetitions than you did the last time.

Sometimes you can practice the movements in slow-motion to pay special attention to the smooth flow of the movement from beginning to end. When performing slowly concentrate on keeping your balance and being precise in your movements.

Sometimes you should practice the movements as fast as possible to build up your speed. Initiate the movement as abruptly as possible, going from compete stillness to sudden top speed. Keep your body relaxed through the movement until you tense at the point of impact. Tensing the muscles (especially of the striking limb) at the point of impact will strengthen the power of the blow.

Learning how to strike with speed is vital. Its importance can hardly be overstated. Slow punches and kicks will simply miss. Your opponent will have time to get out of the way. So the ability to go from being physically still to suddenly striking at top speed is an essential thing to practice.

Some people find it useful to visualise an imaginary opponent when performing the techniques as this helps to "target" the blows. Your punches, kicks, and strikes should be aimed at a specific target on your opponent's body and visualisation is a helpful way of keeping this in mind.

If you have the means to improvise (or purchase) a punchbag or kickbag, it will help a great deal to practice your blows against a bag. It will inform you of how strong or weak your blows are, and it will assist in making them stronger. If you have only ever practiced your techniques against the air, then the first time you use them against a punchbag or kickbag you may be *horrified at how weak* the impact seems to be. This is a salutary lesson. It is a useful reminder that actually hitting someone is very different from just punching and kicking the air. Fighting is not dancing.

So, even if you have to make some kind of homemade punchbag to hit because you can't afford to buy one, it's well worth doing so. Again, repetition is the key. Hit the bag over and over again. Get used to the feeling of the impact against something solid, and work at increasing the power of your blows. (When using a bag you may notice how keeping your body relaxed as you strike and then tensing your muscles at the point of impact really can help to improve power.)

COMBINE TECHNIQUES

Toward the end of this book there are some suggestions for combining simple techniques. This is because you are very unlikely to stop an assailant with a single blow. In a fight you will need to keep fighting until it's over, however long that may take. So you don't just hit an opponent once with a single technique and then pause to examine the effects of your labours thus far. You can't just thump them and stand back as if to admire your handiwork: "There, you see, I can fight too, and what do you think of that?"

By pausing you are giving them a chance to hit you back. Don't stop, keep going. Your goal is to make them stop fighting and go away. If you've started hitting them, then you have to keep on hitting them until they quit and leave you alone, or until you have the chance to run away out of danger. Remember, we're not talking about sport, and we're not talking about an honourable duel between noble gentlemen, we're talking about personal survival.

With this in mind, it's worth mentioning in advance that it's important to remember to breathe. This may sound odd, but it's true. When you're trying to hit someone repeatedly it's surprisingly easy to *unintentionally* hold your breath. You're so busy throwing punches and kicks that *you don't realise* you're holding your breath, and if you make that mistake then you're obviously going to run out of breath really quickly. You'll be pummelling away but then you'll have to stop fighting in order to desperately suck in air. While you're frantically inhaling, you are vulnerable.

So, never mind if you're panting so loud that you sound like a dog on a hot summer's day, that's better than running out of breath. Pant as loud as a steam train if you need to, just make sure than you breathe.

Martial arts such as karate will try to ensure this by teaching the student to exhale forcefully when striking and inhaling between strikes. This is a sensible rule. Exhaling sharply when you hit an opponent helps with the timing of the action (boxers do this too), and it helps to avoid your getting winded if your opponent simultaneously hits you in the torso. Better yet, by deliberately exhaling when you strike, your body should instinctively inhale afterwards as a natural reflex.

It would be beneficial, therefore, to practice exhaling forcefully when you perform these techniques at full speed. In this way you can teach yourself how to breath whilst fighting.

The Front Kick (Figures 4 and 5).

Figure 4

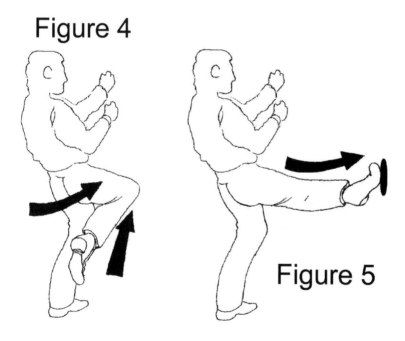

Figure 5

A martial arts front kick is different from the type of kick used when kicking a soccer ball. The soccer kick swings the leg forward and the foot rises upwards. A martial arts front kick lifts the knee high (Figure 4) and then thrusts the foot forward into the target (Figure 5). It's important to pull the toes back so that it is the ball of the foot that hits the target, *not the toes*. When kicking, try to keep your hands raised in front of you to guard your face. Keep the knee of the supporting leg slightly bent for better balance and stability.

In both Figures 6 and 7 the target is the groin but notice how in Figure 6 the foot rises up into the target, striking with the instep of the foot like kicking a soccer ball, whereas in Figure 7 the lifting of the knee puts the foot on the same level as the target and then the foot shoots straight out to strike with the ball of the foot.

Figure 6   Figure 7

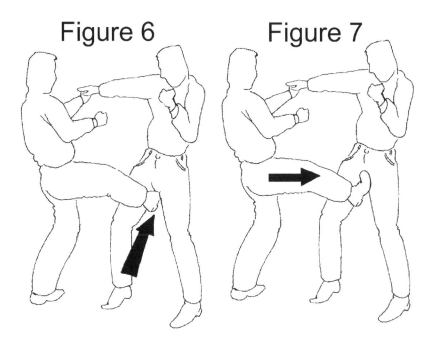

In recommending the front kick with the ball of the foot I am *not* rejecting the soccer kick using the instep. You might use either. But kicking with the instep can only really be used to target the groin because the foot is travelling upwards (so the target must be above it). The martial arts version of the front kick has the advantage that it can be used against multiple targets because the foot travels forward like a punch.

Targets for the front kick

The opponent's shins, knees, and groin are the best targets. Ideally, when kicking the knee the opponent's leg will be straight so that you are kicking *against the joint* (Figure 8).

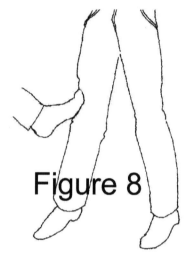

Any strikes against the knee or the elbow will be most effective when they force the joint to bend the "wrong" way.

The stomach is also a possible target for a front kick but it is advisable not to kick too high as this may cause the non-expert to lose their balance, creating the danger of stumbling or falling over. Your opponent might even manage to catch your foot and throw or push you over.

In addition, we should remember that if you're wearing restrictive clothing, this will limit how high you can kick. So as a general rule it would be better to keep your kicks below waist height.

Chapter 5

Men At Risk

The Crime Survey for England and Wales reports that in the year 2011/2012:

"Young men are most likely to be victims of violence . . . Men were nearly twice as likely as women (3.8% compared with 2.1%) to have experienced one or more violent crimes." [The Guardian online, 2013]

"Although it is the attacks on young women that we are most likely to respond to, it is young men who, overwhelmingly, are victims of violence (as the stories of knife attacks over the past year so well illustrate). But their fear is usually hidden . . . Young men are not allowed to display fear because that is a sign of weakness." [The Guardian online, 2008]

Women are constantly being told that they are threatened by a predatory society and that they are in need of greater protection. But how often does society show concern for the physical dangers that threaten its male population? Political campaigns against the amount of violence in society invariably declare that they are opposing "violence *against women*". This slogan specifically *excludes* any concern for male victims. Yet men are actually more likely to suffer violent assault than women. Does a man's pain count for nothing? There is an important truth that needs to be stated loudly and clearly. It is this:

MOST MEN CAN'T FIGHT

That's right, contrary to what the entertainment industry would like you to believe, *most men can't fight*. It's true but everyone seems to want to keep quiet about it. There are several reasons for this secrecy on the subject, none of them very flattering to either sex. Let's consider a few.

(1) Some fools seem to judge their fighting ability on their skill at playing computer games. Their avatar beats the hell out of the other animated characters in the game and the player somehow convinces themselves that this means that they are good at fighting. Many people have no experience of real violence and the closest thing they get to it is watching fight scenes in Hollywood movies or watching Mixed Martial Arts videos on You Tube.

It doesn't matter how many thousands of tough guy movies you've seen, that won't do you any good when three nasty bastards decide to stop you in the street because they want to have some fun kicking your broken ribs into your lungs.

(2) Men think that they're *supposed to be able to fight* and they don't want to admit the embarrassing truth that they can't. This derives, of course, from traditional gender roles.

This age-old misandry is the reason that society cares less about male victims of violence than it cares about female victims. Society is still trading on the false assumption that men *ought* to be able to protect themselves and so *it's their own fault* if they can't. This is sheer sexism. Not being able to fight is still seen as a failure of masculinity, as it has been for countless generations, so it's hardly surprising if men are embarrassed and reluctant to admit it.

But men themselves cannot afford to accept this traditional attitude toward their gender. In matters of personal self-defence, honesty is the best policy. Own up to it, if only to yourself. There is no shame in not knowing how to fight, just be consciously aware of the fact so that you don't walk blithely into trouble that you can't handle.

"No problem, babe, I can handle this little guy."

(3) Women don't want to admit that most men can't fight because they expect men to defend them, especially their boyfriends, and they prefer to just take it for granted that all men are equipped to perform the task of being an impromptu bodyguard whenever one is needed. It's the misandry of those traditional gender roles again. But if women can no longer be expected to know how to cook, then men can no longer be expected to know how to fight.

Listen up girls. You are *not* entitled to expect a man to be your *human shield*. In the past men would put themselves in harm's way to protect a woman, but no longer. After fifty years of feminism telling men how useless and unnecessary they are, it's far too late to demand that men in society should "man up" and act like John Wayne to protect the dainty little damsel in distress.

This applies even more to male strangers than it does to boyfriends. Why should a man who doesn't even know you put himself at risk by rushing to your rescue when you're in a situation of danger? After half a century of feminism's contemptuous rejection of traditional gender roles, how can you possibly demand that men fulfil their traditional gender role of protecting women? All hypocrisy must have its limits.

Men have always had to protect themselves as best they could, including those who didn't know how. These days the same applies to women. The slogan is "A woman needs a man like a fish needs a bicycle". The slogan isn't "A woman needs a man like a fish needs a bicycle *until she needs him to take a beating from some thug in order to keep her safe*". Why should the emasculated men raised in a feminised society sacrifice themselves for the sake of women? Not that they are likely to be capable of defending anyone.

The plain fact is that even in the past most men couldn't fight. Here's a personal anecdote to illustrate what I mean. I once saw two fit young men have a fight at work. It took place in a warehouse. The two guys were both around nineteen years old and they were both in good shape. They were a couple of lean muscular black guys who looked like they'd be pretty dangerous with their fists. But what actually happened was this.

The fight lasted about one and a half minutes, during which time they lashed out at one another with wildly flailing punches and kicks. They leapt about avoiding all these blows, crashing into warehouse crates, making a lot of noise and knocking things over. But from first to last neither of them actually landed a single blow on their opponent. Being young and fit, they were fast. Consequently, neither of them could catch the other. They dodged out of the way of every blow. After a minute and a half they were both completely out of breath and puffing so hard that they stopped fighting. At which point they decided to call it quits. The fight was over without a blow being struck. Neither man had managed to hit his opponent, not even once. That's a true story.

Besides the average man's inability to fight effectively, there is also the issue of men's reluctance to fight. The supposedly innate capacity for "male violence" is hugely exaggerated in regard of most men. The clichés and caricatures of "manhood", both past and present, are not accurate descriptions of ordinary men. Not only is feminism's contemporary gender stereotype of men (as sexually predatory, domestically abusive, patriarchal bullies who oppress women through violence and the threat of violence) a ludicrous misrepresentation of men, the traditional gender stereotype of men was bogus too.

For example, it is a commonplace experience of men in war that they are reluctant to fire upon the enemy, even when under fire themselves. It is not unusual for soldiers armed with "small arms" like rifles to not shoot their weapons in combat or to fire high, deliberately shooting to miss. In his book "Men Against Fire" Brigadier General Samuel Marshall, who was a military analyst for the U.S. Army in World War 2, controversially claimed that:

"of the World War II U.S. troops in actual combat, 75% never fired at the enemy for the purpose of killing, even though they were engaged in combat and under direct threat." [Wikipedia]

To explain this, Marshall argued that the American soldier was a product of:

"a civilization in which aggression, connected with the taking of life, is prohibited and unacceptable . . . The fear of aggression has been expressed to him so strongly and absorbed by him so deeply and pervadingly - practically with his mother's milk - that it is part of the normal man's emotional make-up. This is his great handicap when he enters combat. It stays his trigger finger even though he is hardly conscious that it is a restraint upon him." [HistoryNet 2006]

Marshall is not the only militarist to have noticed this engrained "fear of aggression" and he drew attention to it because, as a Brigadier General, he naturally saw his soldiers' reluctance to kill the enemy as a problem. He wanted the U.S. Army to expend more of their training resources on increasing their soldiers willingness to fire upon the enemy.

I don't mention this to disparage the soldiers. Not at all. A lot of brave men fought in a lot of terrible wars and their service should be acknowledged with respect. But, nonetheless, let's be aware that the ordinary man's behaviour in war wasn't anything like a John Wayne movie. (Ironically, Wayne did not serve in the military during WW2 and some people have accused him of being a "draft-dodger".)

My point is that Marshall is speaking of a conscript army of *ordinary men*, not military-minded volunteers, and if men's "fear of aggression" was a limiting factor in their capacity to fight in the past, then how much greater will that limitation be in today's feminised society?

Men and boys in contemporary society are *actively taught* to fear their own capacity for "male aggression" and "male violence" because these things are seen as social ills; the besetting sins of the alleged Patriarchy. But the truth is that most men have far less capacity for violence than is popularly believed.

Of course, there are individual men (and women) who have a great capacity for violence and they revel in it. But any man who assumes that he can fight simply because he's a man, relying upon some kind of inherent male capacity for violence, is fooling himself. The implications for self-defence are obvious.

"Don't worry, he's a man, he can take care of himself."

Putting Your Weight Behind the Blow

The Basic Punch (Figure 9).

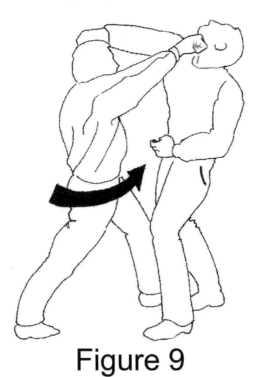

Figure 9

When striking with the fist turn your upper body into the punch, putting the momentum of this rotation of your shoulder and hip behind the punching arm. Make sure that your rear foot is planted firmly on the ground so that you can push the rotation of your torso from the rear leg.

It is important that the fist should be tightly clenched at the moment of impact, otherwise you might damage your fingers. Do not bend your wrist. The striking arm should be a straight line from the shoulder to the knuckles. Do not merely punch *to* the target, attempt to drive your fist *right through* the target.

Circular Elbow Strike (Figure 10).

Figure 10

This is the same movement as described in the basic punch but the elbow strike can be used when you are too close to your opponent to punch effectively. For example, when struggling chest to chest. Keep the striking arm fully bent throughout the movement with the fist close to your own chest. Impact is made with the point of the elbow which is swung round as the torso twists. Targets for this strike are the throat, the side of the jaw, the eye, and the temple.

An alternative to the circular elbow strike is the "hook" punch or "roundhouse" punch (if there is room to pull the arm around in a semi-circular movement) where the arm is bent (but not fully bent) to hit with the fist, targeting the side of the jaw or the temple.

Palm Heel Strike 1 (Figure 11).

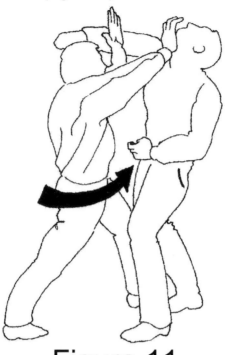

Figure 11

This again employs the same rotation of the upper body seen in the basic punch, turning the torso to put the your shoulder and hip behind the punching arm. The heel of the palm can be used either as a strike or as a push. The fingers should be bent and pulled back so that the fleshy base of the palm can be used as the striking surface to make impact on the target.

The targets are the nose or the chin, with the blow rising from underneath the target to hit upwards (Figure 13). As with punching, do not merely strike *to* the target, attempt to drive the heel of your hand *right through* the target.

When used as a strike the attack is delivered as fast as a punch. But if your opponent has grabbed you in a bear hug, then the same movement can be used as a strong persistent push to break out of the hold.

Palm Heel Strike 2 (Figure 12).

The palm heel can be used with the leading arm too, either as a fast strike or as a strong push to break free from a grappling hold.

But notice that the rotation of the torso is now *in the opposite direction*. The upper body is turned so that the front shoulder and hip are thrust forward behind the attacking arm.

Figure 12

Push off the rear leg to thrust a straight arm forwards and upwards so that there is a more or less straight line from the rear foot to the striking hand. To make the palm heel strike more powerful, grab the wrist of your opponent with your rear hand and pull them towards you as you thrust your striking hand into their nose or chin.

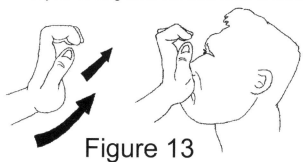

Figure 13

"The Old One-Two" (Figures 14 and 15).

The twisting of the torso in these techniques is what is meant by "putting your weight behind the blow". It is essential if you want to hit hard. You are not merely punching or striking with the hand but rather *with the whole body*. If you watch a boxer hitting a heavy punchbag you will see him twisting his upper body behind each punch.

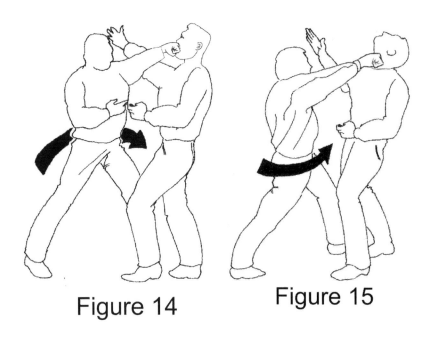

Figure 14   Figure 15

This is seen most clearly in what boxers have long called "the old one-two" where a quick jab with the leading fist is instantly followed by a punch with the rear fist. The classic example of "the old one-two" is a jab to the face (to make your opponent raise his hands to guard his face) followed by punch to the stomach, but it can be used against any targets. For example, you might jab to your opponent's face to knock their head back, followed by a punch to their exposed throat (Figures 14 and 15).

Chapter 6

Women At Risk

I've spent some time addressing the issue that, contrary to conventional attitudes about violence, men are greatly at risk and in need of protection. Now let's address the violence that women face in society. It is equally disturbing. What makes it all the more frightening is that the popular conception of violence perpetrated against a woman portrays her as being in peril from her boyfriend, husband, or the men who are around her every day.

When discussing female victims of violence it is usually emphasized that the women knew their attackers personally and that the greatest danger may lurk in seemingly innocuous circumstances. The attractive man you've just met at a party who gives you a lift home because the streets are not safe might turn out to be the real threat. The same may apply to the taxi driver who collects you from the party. Is it safe to be trapped in a car with him? Is the workman who calls at your house someone that you can trust inside your own home? Did you remember to examine his identification closely enough? Should you work late at the office if it means you'll be alone in the office with a male co-worker? Danger does not always announce itself, it sometimes strikes out of a clear blue sky. The situation may be familiar and commonplace, there may be no prior indication of danger. An apparently mundane situation may change astonishingly quickly into something terribly threatening.

In these circumstances it is worth remembering that, besides the physical self-defence techniques illustrated in this book, it can sometimes be of value to make use of the simplest of all protective measures: screaming. People don't think of shouting as a self-defence technique but it might help with an assailant whose attack is opportunistic and may therefore not be resolutely determined. Your assailant might become afraid himself if you're making a lot of noise. It may not bring anyone to your assistance but he can't be sure of that. He may start worrying about his own safety. He wants you to be quiet so that he can commit his crime undisturbed, so if you're hollering to wake the dead he may fear discovery and abandon his attack.

I'm not suggesting here anything like the feminist-inspired female self-defence videos that have appeared in recent years. In these ridiculous videos a woman is menaced by a man, so she holds up an open hand in a "Stop!" gesture and says "No!" in an assertive manner. This is farcical. It has nothing to do with real violence. No genuine assailant is going to be intimidated by an imperious tone of voice. Any man who stops when he's *told* to stop is not actually an attacker at all, he is simply a pushy individual who's trying his luck.

Someone who intends you serious harm isn't going to be deterred by being spoken to in the manner of a dog owner house-training a puppy. These feminist videos seem to assume that a woman can command all men simply by taking a high hand with them, which may reflect the average feminist's experience of men. But rapists are unlikely to fall into that category of male. No, when I say that a lot of noise might give an attacker second thoughts, I mean continuously screaming the place down at the top of your lungs.

But if this fails, then you must be ruthless in defending yourself. Your conscience is clear; your assailant has forced this violence upon you. At close quarters ruthlessness is essential and once you're committed to using any of the techniques in this book, give it all you've got. Don't hold back. Do as much damage as you can to break free, and then get out of there fast.

However, all of the scenarios mentioned above in which a woman is menaced by someone she knows personally are, as I said, the popular conception of violence against women. It would be a mistake to assume that they are the whole of the potential danger, not least because they presuppose that the woman is facing a threat from a single assailant. Recent events indicate that the hazards to women in society may be getting worse. The rapidly changing demographics of Western Europe appear to have brought shocking new threats. Are the news stories about the mass violence done to women in Germany on New Year's Eve 2015, the orchestrated sexual assaults called *taharrush*, a sign of the times?

"Police fear a gang-rape phenomenon known as 'taharrush' in the Arab world, and seen in attacks on women across German cities at the New Year, has now spread to Europe. The name of the practice translates to 'collective harassment' and is carried out by large groups of men who sexually assault lone women, either by groping, or in some instances, raping them. The men first surround their victim in circles. Some then sexually assault her, while others not directly involved watch or divert outsiders' attention to what is occurring. Sometimes the terrified victim - in a state of shock and unable to respond - is also robbed during the ordeal. And the attack usually goes unpunished because the large number of perpetrators and chaos of the attack means authorities are unable to identify those involved." [Mail Online, January 2016.]

Age is no barrier to the threat of sexual violence. The notorious Rotherham child sex exploitation scandal was only one example, though the most egregious, of organised Muslim rape gangs in England targeting pubescent girls. (There have been many such rape gangs around the country, including in Rochdale, Leeds, Keighley, Aylesbury, Banbury, Bristol, and elsewhere.)

They all follow the same pattern, being networks of men within Muslim communities who sexually groom young and often underage non-Muslim girls. The victims are treated as sex-slaves to be handed around amongst the network of rapists. The police and local government fail to intervene due to their fear of being branded racist.

"At least 300 possible suspects have been identified by investigators probing the Rotherham child sex exploitation scandal. The National Crime Agency (NCA) said most of the potential suspects were Asian men, while the vast majority of victims were young British girls. The NCA launched a major investigation into the scandal after a damning report by Professor Alex Jay last year, revealed that as many as 1,400 children had been raped, trafficked and groomed by mainly Asian gangs in the South Yorkshire town between 1997 and 2013." [The Telegraph online, June 2015]

This would be inconceivable if it hadn't actually happened. Hundreds of suspects and well over a thousand victims in *one town*, in a socially orchestrated series of crimes that continued unabated over the course of sixteen years. And the question is left open: *in how many other towns is this happening?*

The famous quote from LP Hartley says "the past is another country, they do things differently there". Let's remember that the same is also true of the future. *The future is another country, they do things differently there.* These days, as we gaze into our crystal ball, the future is looking extremely uncertain and perilous. There seem to be many potential causes of sweeping increases in public violence in the years to come. Various kinds of "preppers" are preparing for everything from global financial collapse to internecine multicultural wars to widespread gender segregation to a religious Armageddon.

Faced with all this dystopian uncertainty some women may feel the need to learn how to better protect themselves. It's a sensible idea. If you don't do it, who's going to do it for you? Maybe this is the reason you bought this book. Perhaps it's the reason that you're thinking of taking self-defence further by attending a self-defence class to get some hands-on practice and training under an instructor. That's also a good idea, but there are a few considerations you should take into account when selecting a class.

1. Women-only self-defence classes.

Women-only classes are sold on the idea that the students will be more relaxed and less intimidated if there are no men around, and that this will make the classes more productive. Unfortunately, this attitude is self-defeating.

Women do not generally learn self-defence because they are afraid of being attacked by other women. This is not to say there aren't any female thugs in society; there certainly are. Thuggery is not a solely masculine vice. Nonetheless women normally want to learn self-defence in order to defend themselves against *male* assailants, in which case you need to practice with a man.

Techniques that work okay against a 130lb woman may not work so well against a 190lb man. Not only is he 60lbs heavier, he is six inches taller and has a longer reach. So, unless you're only concerned to defend yourself against very small men, a women-only class is not fit for purpose. You don't need to know what works against an obliging female partner in a relaxed environment, you need to know what works (and what doesn't work) against an aggressive male drunk.

Practicing your self-defence techniques with a male partner will provide a more realistic experience of the physical mechanics entailed in attempting to apply them. The importance of this is more than just gaining some experience of applying the techniques to a person the size of a man, it's also a matter of acquiring the confidence of having used them on a person of that size. For a technique to work it has to be applied with confidence and if in a real situation of violence you're facing an assailant who's far larger than anyone you've practiced your techniques with, then this is going to drain all the confidence right out of you.

So, for self-defence purposes it is essential that a woman practices her techniques against a male opponent.

2. The Limitations of Faking It.

Violence, like sex, isn't the same when it's simulated. Bear in mind that, although it does have value, a self-defence class can only offer you a *simulation* of attack and defence.

In class you are being careful not to hurt your training partner and they are trying to avoid hurting you. The punches, kicks, and strikes are not being delivered with full contact. Often these are practiced in class without the punch or kick making contact at all. There is a lot of punching the air. "Attackers" wait patiently with their arms held out while "defenders" practice their technique on a stationary target. In a real fight punches flash out in the blink of an eye. Understandably, self-defence classes can't be truly realistic. You're not really in any danger. There is no element of pain and there is no element of fear. Real fights are painful and scary. You may be great in class but get killed on the street.

The most effective self-defence techniques are likely to be the ones that do the most physical damage to your assailant. But these are the very ones that you can't practice seriously in class. You cannot, for example, safely practice sticking your thumbs into someone's eyes, or breaking someone's finger and then wrenching it around to induce pain. In class, you can only fake it. As a result, there may be a tendency in a formal self-defence class to avoid just those techniques which may be the most valuable.

One thing I would strongly recommend is to pick a self-defence class that incorporates the use of punchbags and focus mitts in their training. It helps considerably to assess the power of your punches and kicks if you actually hit something. This is the great advantage that sports like boxing have over various forms of "no-contact" training. The boxer sparring in the ring not only experiences hitting an opponent but, even more importantly, they experience getting hit by an opponent.

It's worth bearing in mind, too, that street thugs may have prior experience of hitting and being hit as a result of having had previous fights. This is an advantage they have over the innocent law-abiding citizen who may have attended self-defence classes but has no real experience of actual fighting. (On the other hand, an assailant might be nothing more than a fool who thinks he's tougher than he is; there are a lot of wannabe tough guys out there!)

All real life self-defence is a last ditch attempt at survival when everything else has failed. The techniques in this book have been chosen on a criteria of simplicity and effectiveness but, be warned, nobody knows in advance how they will react in a situation of genuine violence. There are no guarantees.

3. Short Courses.

Another drawback of self-defence classes is that they can sometimes foster overconfidence. I said above that it's essential to apply the techniques with confidence, but it's also true that having too much confidence in your abilities can get you into trouble because you're walking around with a false sense of security.

Let's say you attend a six-week course of instruction at the end of which you feel that you've really learned something. Now you feel that you have the knowledge to protect yourself; after all, you've done a course on it! This is not a realistic attitude. Your training only lasted six weeks. Self-defence techniques cannot be learned sufficiently well to be remembered under stress in so short an amount of time. Beware overconfidence. Remember: no one is safe. Self-defence classes do not change this. Certainly not in six weeks.

A good test of what you have actually learned from a self-defence class is to see how well you react *when you don't know what attack is about to be made against you*. The thing is, when practicing in class the instructor will tell the attacking partner to make a specific attack and tell the defending partner how to respond to it. In this way the student learns a number of specific defences to employ against specific attacks. But real fighting is messy and awkward, and you don't know what your assailant is going to do next. So to discover whether the techniques you've learned are likely to work in an actual fight, you need to see whether you can apply them spontaneously when *you don't know in advance* what attack you have to defend against. The results can sometimes be disappointing.

This is especially a problem if the techniques you've been taught include complicated manoeuvres where you "block" and "trap" and "apply pressure" and "throw" your assailant, or anything convoluted like that. It is to avoid the problem of the applicability of complicated techniques in a real life situation that this book features very simple techniques that might apply to *any sort of attack.*

If an assailant rushes at you, then a basic front kick is a serviceable defence. In a fight a basic punch is something that you can use whenever your opponent is within reach. The best techniques to have under your belt are those which have the widest applicability.

For the non-expert it is better to practice half a dozen very basic techniques that can be applied in nearly any situation, rather than to have a whole catalogue of highly specific techniques which *can only be applied against specific attacks.* As I said in Chapter 1, the problem is *reaction time.* In the chaotic mess of a real fight, by the time you've thought of which specific technique you should have used against an attack, it's too late and you've already been hit.

I'm not trying to dissuade anyone from attending a self-defence class. On the contrary, I think they're a good idea. But, if you attend one, try to be aware which of the techniques that they teach you are honestly *likely to work in a real fight* and which are cool-looking martial arts moves that you'd wisely never dare to attempt if your life depended upon it.

4. Self-Defence / Martial Arts.

A distinction should be drawn between self-defence classes and martial arts classes. The study of a martial art is necessarily a long-term undertaking and it will entail learning things that are not of immediate use as self-defence. This is not to say that martial arts aren't a good way of learning how to defend yourself, it's simply to point out that any system of martial arts expects the student to devote themselves to diligent practice over a long period of time. There are no shortcuts in the martial arts. Therefore, they may not serve the more short-term needs of the non-expert who wants to acquire some ability to defend themselves straight away.

Moreover, a lot of what makes a martial art so enjoyable and interesting is the aesthetic aspect of the physical discipline. In other words, a lot of the pleasure comes from the "art" not just from the "martial". I would certainly recommend the martial arts (I gave a decade of my life to karate) but you should appreciate that it's about more than just self-defence.

One benefit you can get fairly quickly from a martial arts class is an improvement in your strength and fitness where you need it most for self-defence; in your ability to punch and kick, etc. This in itself is very valuable for the purpose of learning to protect yourself.

Sideways Elbow Strike (Figure 16)

This is used when you are standing sideways to your opponent and are close enough to reach him with your elbow. (It could, for example, be useful if you are sitting in a car with your assailant sitting next to you.)

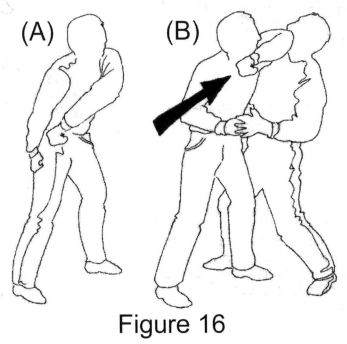

Figure 16

Your arm begins across your torso with the hand near your opposite hip (Figure 16A). Bring the elbow diagonally up towards your opponent's face with your arm bending as your elbow rises. The targets are the eye, the nose, the temple, or the throat. The strike is made with the point of the elbow. On impact your arm should be fully bent with your hand near, or underneath, your own chin (Figure 16B).

To maximize the power of the strike, *lean into* the attack as your elbow rises into the target. When performed standing, this technique begins by pushing off the rear foot to put the weight of your body behind the strike.

Back Kick (Figures 17 and 18)

An assailant may attack you from behind. It is therefore useful to be able to kick to the rear. The back kick can be the most powerful of kicks (it is sometimes called a "donkey kick" due to its resemblance to the way that donkeys kick out backwards) but it has the disadvantage that you can't see your opponent very well. You will need to turn your head as you kick if you wish to see your target. Otherwise you will be kicking back blindly (which may sometimes be necessary but is not ideal).

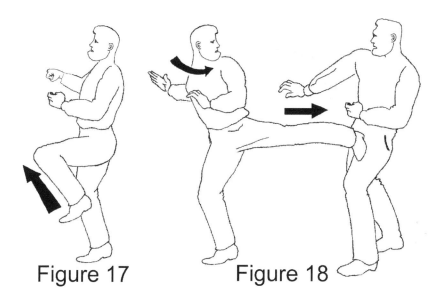

Figure 17   Figure 18

Raise the knee of your kicking leg (Figure 17) and then kick *directly backwards* in a straight line (Figure 18). It is a strong thrusting movement. Make impact with the heel of your foot. Do not let your kicking leg stray to the left or to the right. The line of the movement should be a dead straight thrust to a target directly behind you.

Targets for the back kick can include anything from the shins to the face, but it is a good general rule for the non-expert to avoid high kicks so the primary targets are your assailant's shins, knees, groin, and belly.

Back Kick When Held (Figure 19)

This is a technique that can be used to escape when you are grabbed and held from behind. Raise your knee (Figure 19A) and then kick down and backwards with your heel (Figure 19B) into the assailant's shin, or stamp downwards with your heel into the assailant's foot. If your opponent does not release his grip on you, kick again repeatedly. If necessary, you can kick alternately with both legs.

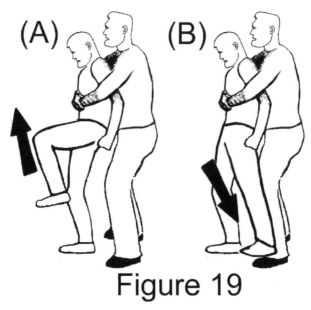

Figure 19

If this successfully causes the assailant to release his grip, then this technique can be combined with the *sideways elbow strike* (Figure 16 above). As soon as your assailant's hold on you loosens, turn sideways toward him and perform the elbow strike upwards into his face or throat. If you continue turning until you are facing your opponent, you could follow up with a basic punch or a front kick. Use the momentum of turning to put your weight behind the blow.

If the assailant releases his grip and steps back, then this technique can be followed up with the thrusting back kick (Figure 18 above) to drive him further away.

Chapter 7

Domestic Violence

"The battered woman defense is a defense used in court that the person accused of an assault/murder was suffering from battered person syndrome at the material time. Because the defense is most commonly used by women, it is usually characterised in court as *battered woman syndrome* or *battered wife syndrome*. There is currently no medical classification for this specific syndrome in the sense used by lawyers, though it has historically been invoked in court systems. Similar to an insanity plea, battered person syndrome is purely a legal term used to refer to the severe psychological trauma caused by domestic abuse." [Wikipedia]

I began the previous chapter by saying that it is usually emphasized that female victims of violence generally know their attackers personally. However, in regard of the method of self-defence featured in this book, there is a big difference between the types of violence that the law calls "domestic violence" or "intimate partner violence" and a violent situation in which the woman simply "knows her assailant".

The basic premise of this book is that you, the non-expert, are the innocent victim of someone else's violence. I am taking it for granted that you are defending yourself against an assault by a clearly guilty perpetrator who has forced this situation of violence upon you. In other words, I am taking the moral issue of who is responsible for the violence as unambiguous and uncontentious. You have not sought this violent encounter and you have tried everything you can to avoid the necessity of fighting but your assailant has left you with no other choice.

I would therefore suggest that the self-defence techniques in this book are not a suitable response to domestic/intimate partner violence (unless the attack is definitely and immediately life threatening). This unsuitability derives primarily from the moral issue of responsibility. The personal relationships within which incidents of domestic violence take place can frequently be so confused and multilayered that it is not a straightforward instance of self-defence.

For example, the question might be asked: didn't you have the opportunity to leave the relationship and thereby avoid the violence? But anyone who knows anything about domestic violence will know that such a question is often overly simplistic. What if the abused person is a father who didn't feel able to leave the family home because he wouldn't be allowed custody of his children and he didn't want to leave them defenceless in the custody of their violent mother? What if the two people in the relationship are both violent toward each another and there is no clear distinction between the abuser and the abused? Domestic violence can be a minefield of complications that cloud the moral issues.

Tragically, this complexity is not reflected in the mainstream view of intimate partner violence. On the contrary, society employs extremely crude gender stereotypes of male guilt and female innocence. These are so entrenched in the way that some people view abusive relationships that there is an extreme divergence between what society and the law considers to be self-defence for women and self-defence for men.

A famous/notorious legal case (in the UK in 1989) was that of Kiranjit Ahluwalia who set fire to her husband while he slept in bed. He was burned to death. She claimed to be acting in self-defence after years of violent abuse. Initially she was convicted of murder but after a feminist campaign in her support the conviction was overturned and declared a mistrial in 1992. She was released. Ahluwalia became a heroine for feminists and a movie based on her life was made in 2006. It's title was "Provoked".

There was a similar case (in Canada in 1977) when Francine Hughes used gasoline to set fire to her ex-husband's bed

60

while he slept. He was killed and the whole house burned down in the fire. She had told her four children to wait in the car and, after starting the fire, she drove to the police station and confessed to the killing. At her trial her defence was that she had suffered many years of domestic violence from her ex-husband. She was found not guilty by reason of temporary insanity. Hughes' story was also made into a movie entitled "The Burning Bed" (1984).

So is setting fire to someone while they're sleeping an act of self-defence? Some people clearly believe that it is (although, we might suspect, *only* if a *woman* does it). But if killing someone in their sleep can be considered a justifiable act of self-defence, then anything can be. And apparently it is:

"Nicole Doucet wanted her estranged husband dead. In September 2007, her thoughts turned to murder. Although the couple had been separated for months and lived 180 kilometres apart in rural Nova Scotia, Ms. Doucet would later testify in her trial that she feared Michael Ryan. She would claim that she had no alternative but to have him killed. Her trial judge agreed.

Ms. Doucet had put out a contract: $25,000 for Mr. Ryan's life. She found a local man to do the job, but he just took the cash and demanded more. So in March 2008, Ms. Doucet tried again, making a deal with another tough guy .
. . . . That hit man was an undercover RCMP officer. Their discussions were video-recorded. Ms. Doucet was arrested and charged with counselling to commission a murder, a very serious crime indeed. A conviction seemed certain. Ms. Doucet signed an agreed statement of facts just before her trial in December 2009, in which she acknowledged her attempts to have her estranged husband killed. But she pleaded not guilty, claiming she had been under duress at the time of the offence.

She alleged in court that Mike Ryan was an abusive, violent husband. For nearly 15 years he had bullied her, threatened her . . . . But she kept all of these incidents and concerns to herself, never breathing a word to anyone until her husband began a relationship with another woman six years ago.

Despite conflicting accounts that Ms. Doucet gave to police and others, despite the lack of any photographs, police evidence, or third-party corroboration, and despite evidence that called into question her credibility, Justice David Farrar of the Nova Scotia Supreme Court accepted the story. Furthermore, he came to the remarkable conclusion her actions in contracting murder were entirely justified. "A reasonable person," the judge decided, "would have acted in the same manner." To the astonishment of legal experts, Mike Ryan, the RCMP and the Crown, Ms. Doucet was acquitted." [National Post, June 2013]

So in Canada, it seems, hiring a hit man to murder your estranged husband who lives 180 kilometres away constitutes an act of self-defence because you had no alternative but to have him killed. The crude gender stereotypes of male guilt and female innocence are deeply entrenched indeed, especially in the judiciary.

But leaving aside the absurdities of the Canadian legal system, what makes it so difficult to judge what constitutes self-defence in domestic violence cases is that personal relationships are muddled and ambiguous. The stark contrasts of "he said / she said" are so dependent upon subjective testimony that it leaves us confused and uncertain as to what really happened. Consequently, people will often make judgements prompted by their own personal prejudices. Yet for an example of the ambiguity within relationships and the inadequacy of conventional ideas about gendered violence, consider the following:

"When a woman killed her abusive husband out of self-defense, she found out that 'he' was actually a woman wearing a prosthetic penis. Angelo Heddington and Elizabeth Rudavsky from Canada had a whirlwind romance, which was followed by a shotgun wedding after four months of dating, and then escalating domestic violence.

But when a battered 27-year-old Elizabeth stabbed Angelo, 30, after he attacked her in 2003, it was the paramedics who discovered a prosthetic penis under 'his' clothes on the way to the hospital." [Mail online, December 2012]

Sometimes, of course, a case of domestic violence is clear and uncontentious. For example, there may be independent testimony from witnesses or there may be copious physical evidence. Some cases may leave very little room for doubt as to who is the guilty party, as when a small child is badly beaten or killed by an adult. But it would be irresponsible and potentially very unjust to treat the general issue of self-defence used in response to domestic violence as if it were as clear-cut in its moral considerations as, say, an innocent pedestrian being attacked by a mugger on the street at night. Nor is it a gender issue.

It is an open secret that there is far more domestic violence in lesbian relationships than is popularly supposed. The "National Intimate Partner and Sexual Violence Survey, 2010 Findings on Victimisation by Sexual Orientation" (published 2013) included statistics that might surprise some people. The lifetime prevalence of violence by an intimate partner was *43.8% for lesbians* compared to *35.0% for heterosexual women*. On these figures lesbians are more likely to suffer domestic violence than straight women. Another interesting figure arising from this research is that 78.5% of bisexual men identified only *females* as the *perpetrators* of the intimate partner violence that they had suffered. [National Center for Injury Prevention and Control of the Centers for Disease Control and Prevention, 2013]

The reality is that domestic violence is a crime committed by people against people. Women commit it against men, men commit it against women, women commit it against women, and men commit it against men. The quaint old-fashioned notion that it is a straight male crime perpetrated against women has long since been debunked. Even governments will admit this these days, although that admission is seldom given proper recognition in law.

"Data from Home Office statistical bulletins and the British Crime Survey show that men made up about 40% of domestic violence victims each year between 2004-05 and 2008-09 . . . . In 2006-07 men made up 43.4% of all those who had suffered partner abuse in the previous year, which rose to 45.5% in 2007-08 . . . . Similar or slightly larger numbers of men were subjected to severe force in an incident with their partner, according to the same documents. The figure stood at 48.6% in 2006-07, 48.3% the next year and 37.5% in 2008-09, Home Office statistics show." [The Guardian online, September 2010.]

Socially (and therefore legally) it is much more difficult for male victims of domestic violence in need of protection from a female perpetrator to claim that they were acting in self-defence when they hit back. If a male victim of domestic violence were to defend himself with the techniques in this book, the law would come down on him like a ton of bricks. A woman might get away with it legally (not least because she could receive the public support of feminist activists), but *morally* if the techniques are not suitable for the male victim, then they are not suitable for the female victim either. The law may be prejudiced but we don't have to be.

"Research showing that women are often aggressors in domestic violence has been causing controversy for almost 40 years, ever since the 1975 **National Family Violence Survey** by sociologists Murray Straus and Richard Gelles of the Family Research Laboratory at the University of New Hampshire found that women were just as likely as men to report hitting a spouse and men were just as likely as women to report getting hit. The researchers initially assumed that, at least in cases of mutual violence, the women were defending themselves or retaliating. But when subsequent surveys asked who struck first, it turned out that women were as likely as men to initiate violence - a finding *confirmed by more than 200 studies* of intimate violence." [Time Magazine online, June 2014]

One crucial factor regarding the use of self-defence techniques against domestic violence is that the defender lives with their assailant. A "hit and run" policy of self-defence doesn't fit this model of violent assault because the assailant may still be there the next day. There are "refuges" available to female victims but there are almost none available to male victims. Either way it is problematic to leave your assailant behind. You may well have to deal with them again in the future. The use of physical self-defence techniques may even exacerbate the level of violence in the relationship.

"Arrest him, officer. I'm the victim!"

So a strategy for self-defence in an abusive personal relationship might require a very different approach from the one taken in this book. Violence in a relationship is likely to develop over a period of time; a series of incidents of increasing seriousness. The time to deal with such behaviour is, of course, *before* things have gone too far. Do not put up with them until you are in fear of your life. Nip them in the bud.

The most suitable response to domestic violence is to report the incidents to the police as soon as a pattern of violence has established itself. You need to get the matter officially on record, as this will be of great importance in any subsequent legal proceedings. Again, this is more difficult for men because they are more likely to be *disbelieved*, and they may find themselves being falsely counter-accused by the female perpetrator (who will likely be *believed* simply because she is a woman). But, even so, early reporting is the sensible approach especially if you have visible injuries. Do not try to "tough it out". Stoicism is not a virtue when the danger is living with you in your own home.

Intimate partner violence can be symptomatic of a broken relationship as well as the cause of one. Whilst some instances of domestic violence will have one person who is unequivocally guilty, other instances may be far more complex as to where the guilt lies (or is shared). Physical self-defence techniques are not the most constructive way of dealing with an immensely difficult situation. The legality of a physical response may also be highly problematic, particularly for male victims. In the heat of the moment you might feel that a physical response is absolutely necessary (as it may be, and only you can judge the level of danger entailed in an attack upon you) but remember that you will have to live with the consequences.

Combining Simple Techniques

The non-expert should avoid complicated techniques but it is still possible to *combine two or three simple strikes*. For

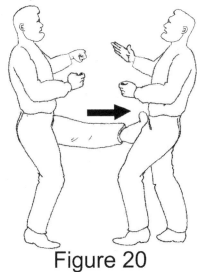

example, one possible combination is to attack your assailant with a basic front kick (Figure 20), then step in with a jab using the leading hand (Figure 21), followed by a basic punch (Figure 22).

Notice that this combination varies the height of the target in each strike to confuse your opponent. It begins with a low target, then switches to a high target, and then finishes with a middle target.

Figure 20

Figure 21

Figure 22

Figure 23

An advantage of using only simple techniques is that they can be applied singly and, if the blow is successful, it can be immediately followed by another simple technique.

In this example of a possible combination the palm heel strike into the assailant's nose or chin is used to break their hold on you (Figure 23) and it is then followed immediately with a "hook" punch to the jaw or the temple (Figure 24).

The hook punch sends the fist in a semi-circle, using a bent arm, so that the movement is forward and across. The blow lands from the side, travelling from right to left (or left to right).

When using these simple techniques in combinations, always twist your upper body to put your weight behind each blow.

Figure 24

Chapter 8

Legal Implications

Want a legal opinion? Ask a lawyer. Maybe they'd be able to give you an accurate account of the laws regarding self-defence in the country that you live in, but I doubt it. It's a sad fact of life that, where the law is concerned, nobody seems to know the answers to the questions you might wish to ask. As a result, if you defend yourself against a violent assault you might find yourself having to defend yourself a second time against another frightening adversary: the judicial system.

Having suffered the attack personally you know (or you think you know) precisely what happened and how it felt. You were accosted, terrified, victimized. You felt the assailant's hands at your throat and the nauseous sensation of panic seizing you. You struck out to protect yourself, blindly, ferociously, in desperation and fear. You were the one who had to make that split second decision in defence of your life, with no time to think and everything at stake. You know perfectly well that you had no choice and your attacker only got what was coming to them. But will a court of law see it that way?

As some people have found to their cost, *innocence* is not necessarily a defence against the law. Your attacker has the same legal rights that you do. Perhaps there were no witnesses to the attack, or perhaps the only "witnesses" were the assailant's friends who will lie through their teeth under oath. If your assailant has suffered physical injuries and is telling his lawyer that you attacked him, you may not be able to prove otherwise. It may be your word against his and the court may decide to believe him, especially if his friends are willing to perjure themselves.

And these days we have trial by media and social media, where people are judged not on the evidence but in accordance with "identity politics". In Florida USA (in February

2012) a violent altercation took place between Trayvon Martin and George Zimmerman in which Martin was shot dead. This was the spark that subsequently led to the national, and to some extent international, "Black Lives Matter" campaign.

Zimmerman claimed self-defence, and Florida is one of the American states which have a "Stand Your Ground" law. This entitles a person to protect and defend their own life against a threat or a perceived threat. It means that a person has *no duty to retreat* from any place they lawfully have a right to be. They may use force, including lethal force, if they reasonably believe that they face an immediate threat of serious bodily harm.

In complete contrast, some other states in the USA have a "Duty To Retreat" law which requires that anyone claiming self-defence as their justification for violence must prove that they had taken reasonable steps to retreat (thereby demonstrating that they had tried to avoid violence) before they used force to defend themselves. So in America the law regarding self-defence isn't even consistent from one state to another.

When Michael Brown was shot by a police officer in Missouri USA (in 2014) it generated widespread civil disorder and a great amplification of the Black Lives Matter campaign. This was despite the fact that the police officer was responding to a theft which Brown had just committed, which led to an altercation when Brown tried to take the police officer's gun from him. The point seized upon by the campaigners as being most significant was that Brown was unarmed when he was shot, although he was advancing toward the officer. On the evidence, the court found that the police officer shot Brown in self-defence. But the media was more inclined to find him guilty.

Of course, these are high-profile cases involving firearms, but they do demonstrate how the laws regarding self-defence vary from place to place, and how the facts of the case do not necessarily settle the matter. At least, not as far as public opinion is concerned. It will be a similar sort of legal system that judges us if we are involved in a fist fight outside our local convenience store. There may not be any guns involved but all self-defence techniques are potentially fatal if delivered strongly enough.

So does that mean you should *not* defend yourself and suffer a brutal beating (or worse) for fear of the legal repercussions? No. The premise of his book is that self-defence is for situations in which you have *no choice*. They are extreme measures for extreme circumstances. They are not to be used to initiate violence. They are not a first recourse but a last ditch effort.

The law judges these things retrospectively, arguing over the evidence in the ceremonial rituals of the criminal court. But the victim had to make *their* judgement at the time when the confrontation was taking place. When violence starts no one, not even the assailant, can know for certain what the outcome will be. Maybe it'll be a bruised eye and a cut lip, or maybe your skull is thinner than you realised and it will fracture. That kick in the ribs might crack them, or it might puncture a lung.

There is no way to be sure what level of violence the assailant will employ before you actually suffer it. Afterwards, it is too late, you're already choking on your own blood and teeth, or clutching at the shards of glass that have lacerated your face. When it's a matter of life and death you cannot think of the possible legal consequences should you survive. In the end, it is better to be prosecuted than paralysed.

The law exists (theoretically at least) to protect you from the criminal acts of other people. It would be great if the law were able to do that. However, the reality is that the representatives of the law are unlikely to be around when you need them. When you are threatened you will probably be terrifyingly alone. *So look after yourself.*

Oh, and since we're talking about legal implications there is one more thing that I'd like to say before the end of this book:

Disclaimer

The author wishes to make it clear that he disclaims all responsibility for the actual use of any of the self-defence techniques featured in this book. As has been repeatedly emphasized, these techniques are extremely dangerous and the consequences of their use would be very serious indeed. Should the reader ever be in a position in which he/she judged the use of these techniques to be justified, the reader must consider himself/herself to be solely responsible for that decision and for his/her own actions.

Good luck and take care. It's a dangerous world out there.

THE END

From the Same Publisher

Available in Paperback

Two "red pill" novels by JP Tate

The Identity Wars

Where will you be in the year 2035? Most novels about a dystopian future have little to do with the real world. They either take place in some post-apocalypse wasteland that has no connection with the present day, or they are old-fashioned visions of far-right totalitarianism on the out-of-date 20th century model.

"The Identity Wars" is very different. It is a new type of dystopian novel based upon the actual society that we live in today. It portrays a dystopian future which arises directly out of the politics and policies of contemporary society.

This novel puts together three features of your world. (1) An impending, and much predicted, serious crash of capitalism causing economic collapse. (2) Western societies becoming ever more divided by multiple ethnic cultures. (3) The growing gender segregation of men and women, such as the social phenomenon of Men Going Their Own Way (MGTOW), as a result of the iniquities of feminism.

Given these three features of the world you live in, "The Identity Wars" looks twenty years into the future and asks: what will society become? *What will happen to a feminist-multiculturalist society under the impact of a global financial meltdown?*

It is also the story of three men on their fortieth birthdays. The grandfather, Alf Eldridge, who was forty in 1975. The father, Michael Eldridge, who was forty in 2005. The son, Kyle Eldridge a.k.a. Ritzy, who is forty in 2035. Each of them is a product of the culture they live in. Each of them lives in a culture entirely different from the other two. Each of them has a wholly different conception of manhood. Across these three generations, from grandfather to grandson, the world changed radically and dramatically. There will be no going back.

This is the news from tomorrow. The future is coming.

The Most Hated Man

A series of bloody deaths is causing panic in a city in England. Someone is murdering teenagers among the underclass by disseminating a lethal recreational drug which, with morbid humour, the mainstream media have termed 'snuff'. But is the snuff-killer just some crazy drug dealer who is pushing a deadly narcotic regardless of the consequences or is he killing these young people deliberately for some deeper motivation of his own?

Two police officers, Detective Inspector Bapoto Smith and Detective Sergeant Gloria Kovač, are a part of the task force unit working the case. Lacking any forensic evidence or public support, they must pursue their investigation hindered further by the puerile restraints of the political directives, policies, and procedures that make up modern policing priorities.

At the same time a second murderer, Hereward, is on a deadly mission of his own. Hereward is abducting members of the political and cultural establishment. For fifty years these reactionaries of 'correctness' have adamantly refused to listen to anyone who disagreed with them. Now Hereward is *making* them listen. The corpses of those to whom he speaks are subsequently found dead by dehydration, bruised from the chains which had bound them. Confronted with this terror the ruling elite are frantic.

Two killers, two fatal agendas, two harassed cops, one broken nation. In a society spiralling out of control, the establishment elites have been targeted and their time is running out.

These storylines slowly come together in a chilling vision of the social alienation brought about by those who exercise authoritarian power over the ordinary citizen with the strict speech-codes and thought-police taboos of political conformity. Set against a background of economic decline, the rise of Islamic Jihad, and the social engineering imposed by the ideologies of multiculturalism and feminism, "The Most Hated Man" is unlike any other cops-and-killers thriller you have ever read. It is a story for our times.

The JP Tate website

http://jptate.jimdo.com

32234749R00044

Printed in Great Britain
by Amazon